Unmasking the Great Pretender

Breaking Bonds of Shame, Living Free!

Linda Forster

Unmasking the Great Pretender
Copyright © 2016 by Linda Forster

ISBN: 978-1-935765-17-2

Covenant of Peace Ministries
Phone: 717-648-4231
www.covofpeace.org

Scripture quotations are taken from The Amplified Bible, Copyright 1965 by Zondervan Publishing and The New American Standard Bible, Copyright 1971 by The Lockman Foundation

Table of Contents

Foreword

Shame is insidious. It's deeply rooted. It underlies much of human behavior. It's in all of us to a certain degree. It's part of our fallen nature, not to mention how we may have picked it up in our journey through life. We've often lived with it so long it's hard to recognize—even if we were brave enough to look directly at it.

To live in the freedom Jesus died to give us and run fully in God's destiny for us, we all, at some point, must confront the shame which lives within us. Not to do so, not to look at, confront, despise and release the shame which Jesus took to the Cross for us means we carry a burden, coloring and distorting our relationships. It also creates a false grid through which we view God, life, and our destiny.

Yes, there is a healthy guilt and shame we need to feel when we have said or done something to ourselves or another which sends a "you are deficient message." When we miss the mark of acting out of unconditional love like Jesus, then guilt and shame are useful in moving us to repentance and restitution toward the offended. They are only intended to move us back into right relationship with God, self and others, not carried and incorporated into our belief system.

The topic for this book is about unhealthy shame—what it looks, feels, and acts like. We will look at its effects—mentally, emotionally, physically and spiritually. Included is new research in the related area of trauma (often intertwined with shame) which underscores how detrimental toxic shame is to us. Lastly, we take on the practicality of ridding ourselves of toxic shame because of what Jesus did for us at the Cross.

Eradicating toxic shame is crucial for us to be overcomers, fulfill our destiny, and advance the Kingdom of God.

Join me on the journey.

Chapter One

In the Beginning....

"...[they] were naked and unashamed."
Genesis 2:25 NASB

There is an impostor in your life! One who pretends. One who hides. One who uses unhealthy behaviors to prevent others from seeing and knowing the "real" you. One who creates and keeps you in a cycle of internal war about who you really are. One who sabotages self, relationships, and life--the life and destiny God created for you. One you may not even know or are willing to admit is there.

Incredible? Impossible? Where did this impostor come from? Why? What can be done? Answering these questions will put you on a path to reclaim the life God intended for you and Jesus died on the Cross to give you.

Who is this impostor? It is the false identity built from shame, which seeks to hide who you believe yourself to be. It is created from believing the lie, "I am fatally flawed, undeserving or worthy of love, belonging, and acceptance."

However, the truth is you were born for love-- hardwired biologically, neurologically, mentally and

7

emotionally for loving, supportive relationships. That is our design, our inheritance, if you will. Loving relationship with God, ourselves and others is the basic foundation of how the Kingdom of God is spread, using our individual gifts and talents divinely deposited in each of us.

When you look around, nurturing, caring, lasting relationships seem the exception rather than the rule. Read any information source out there today and the brokenness in relationship is starkly evident, not only for individuals, but within families, communities, cities, states, and nations.

What gets relationships off track and what makes them so difficult at times? What causes us to long for relationship on the one hand while pushing it away with the other? Why do people hide who they are behind facades of shyness, bragging, anger, denial, or any other number of ways? What bedrock fractures in and of human relationship govern not only our interactions with others but the torment or the joy of life?

Shame, along with fear, are two of the master emotions and tactics which the enemy uses to help us build this pretender, this impostor, in our lives. When in operation, shame and fear steal our identity and derail us from our destiny. While this book focuses on shame, please note that fear drives thoughts and actions which result in shame. Understanding these two powerful and foundational tactics of the enemy in life, learning how to recognize them, how the enemy uses them in your life, and how to resolve them will restore peace, joy, and purpose. And, quite possibly, restore health to your body.

Genesis, the book of beginnings, relates the outset of shame and fear--so we begin there.

Genesis 1:26 tells us that God created the human[1] in "our image, after our likeness." Matthew Henry comments on this verse, "Man was to be a creature different from all that had been hitherto made. Flesh and spirit, heaven and earth, must be put together in him, and he must be allied to both worlds." Henry further states that God's image in the [hu]man (addition mine) is found in three areas, nature and constitution (soul, not the body), in His place and authority ("...let him have dominion", Genesis 1:26), and in His purity and righteousness.[2]

The Bible tells us, "....for thou hast created all things, and **for thy pleasure** (desire, will) **they are and were created.**" Revelation 4:11. (Emphasis mine.) In Proverbs 8:31, "Wisdom" (commentators agree this is referring to Jesus)[3] is speaking of God and says, "...and having my delight in the sons of men." That word delight in Hebrew means bent toward, inclined to, to take intensive pleasure in.[4] Man was created, then, for the desire and will of God and He takes intense pleasure in the sons of men. How, then, does God receive pleasure from us?

---

[1] The actual word in Hebrew is human. This is significant because the first human was male and female, since Eve was taken out of Adam. Humanity is only complete and fully representative of the Godhead and relationship when both male and female are present, fulfilling their equal but complementary roles. www.Scripture4all.org/OnlineInterlinearOTpdf/gen1.pdf
[2] Matthew Henry, *Commentary on Genesis 1*, https://www.blueletterbible.org/Comm/mhc/Gen/Gen_001.cfm.
[3] www.biblehub.com and www.blueletterbible.org, various commentaries
[4] James Strong, LL.D, S.T.D. *The New Strong's Exhaustive Concordance of the Bible,* (Thomas Nelson Publishers. Nashville, TN. 1990), Hebrew #8191.

Since the [hu]man is created in the image and likeness of God and God is love (I John 4:8), we are designed in our spirit, soul, and body to receive and give love. We are created for nurturing and loving relationship, spiritually, mentally, emotionally, socially, even physiologically.[5] God receives pleasure and the fulfillment of His desire for creating us when we reciprocate His love.

Because love cannot be forced or it is not love, one aspect of how we are created in His likeness is our free will. God loves us because that is His nature. We are given freedom to choose to love God back. Our design by God to be loved and give love also extends to love and relationship with ourselves and others. Experientially knowing (*ginosko* [Greek], to know through personal experience)[6] and living out the love relationship with God in our lives demonstrates the reality of the Godhead, which furthers His Kingdom, through our relationship with ourselves and others.

God placed the [hu]man in the Garden of Eden which He also created. In Hebrew, Eden means pleasure or delight.[7] Out of His nature (love), God established a perfect environment, a place of pleasure and delight, for His highest creation in which to dwell, in whom He takes intense pleasure.

God saw there was no created counterpart[8] (a helper for what is needed) to the [hu]man. He then put the

---

[5] Much research in the last 25-30 years has confirmed that we are wired for relationship in every part of our being. See bibliography.

[6] Strong, Greek #1097

[7] Strong, Hebrew numbers 5730; 5731.

[8] The original Hebrew transliterated is "as in front of him." www.Scripture4all.org/OnlineInterlinearOTpdf/gen1.pdf

[hu]man into a deep sleep and took a rib from the [hu]man, separating the female from the male, creating woman. Both lived in, and were caretakers of, the Garden. There God fellowshipped with Adam and Eve, giving and receiving the pleasure that authentic relationship (love) requires.

Truly, it was an idyllic existence, fellowshipping with God in the cool of the day with an environment created to delight and sustain every need of Adam, Eve, and the created beings. Genesis 2:25 gives a glimpse of life there—they were naked and not ashamed. There was no covering and hiding of themselves physically or emotionally. There was no need.

God put everything in the Garden, save one, at their disposal. His one instruction to Adam (before Eve was taken out of him) was, "And the Lord God took the [hu]man and put him in the garden of Eden to tend and guard *and* keep it. And the Lord God commanded the [hu]man, saying, 'You may freely eat of every tree of the garden, except of the tree of the knowledge of good and evil *and* of blessing and calamity you shall not eat, for in the day that you eat of it you shall surely die.'" (Genesis 2:15-17 AMP). Seems simple enough. What could go wrong?

Genesis 3 opens with the description of the serpent as subtle, crafty, shrewd, or sly—more so than any of the other creatures. His interaction with Eve was designed to cast doubt (a subtle form of fear) on the nature and character of God. The serpent challenged the truth of what God had told Adam by telling Eve she will not die if she eats from the tree of the knowledge of good and evil. He created enough doubt and subtly appealed to her mortal (weak, frail) nature, telling her she could exist (be) like

God. So she took from the tree, ate of its fruit and gave it to her husband, who also ate.

Eating from the tree was a direct act of disobedience to God resulting in a shift in awareness of, and perception of, themselves, God, life and the world around them. Immediately, Scripture says, their eyes were opened, they knew they were naked, and sewed fig leaves together to cover their loins. They were now hiding themselves from each other and from God.

When God comes to meet with them, He must call to find them. In response to God's call Adam said, "...I heard the sound of You in the garden, and I was afraid because I was naked; so I hid myself." (Genesis 3:10).

Why is this story so important? Because there is a principle in Bible interpretation called "first mention." When a word or concept is first introduced in Scripture, it is to be used as a basis for interpretation or explanation of further "mentions." This story is key to understanding how fear and shame work together and have become the two master strategies of the enemy.

Although not directly mentioned, when the serpent questions the character and nature of God to Eve, creating doubt, fear is inferred by the actions which follow. Perhaps they believed God was holding out on them and they were missing something that would make them like God. Whatever the thought process, they perceived a lack. Instead of waiting to talk to God about their lack, they used their free will, attempting to solve the issue, causing them to choose disobedience and sin. What followed was shame as evidenced by covering themselves and hiding from God.

Notice the progression, fear of some kind causes us to doubt the character and nature of God. When fear is allowed control in us, then most often the choice made from the fear is a sinful one. Once we have sinned, shame comes whether or not we recognize it. Shame causes us to hide out of fear—and the cycle continues. Because of the link between sin and shame, shame, like sin, is an inherent part of our nature. Dake's Annotated Reference Bible states, "Without sin, there is no shame."[9]

Since God created and designed us for love and relationship, to be known and to know others at a deep level emotionally, it makes perfect sense why the enemy uses shame. Shame in conjunction with fear, as we saw in Genesis, destroys the very thing for which we are created.

Satan's strategy worked and since then his tactics have remained the same. He will do whatever he can to manipulate the weakness of our flesh. Giving place to fear and shame starts a process of broken relationship with God, ourselves and others. Genesis 3:7-8, 12, demonstrates this brokenness. They first covered themselves, hiding from each other (v.7), secondly they hid from God (v.8), finally progressing to accusation and blame as the "cover up."

Sadly, this progression is repeated endlessly within ourselves and others. It brings a harvest of bitter fruit, leaving us at war with God and truth, with who God created us to be, and at war with others. Destroying relationship is the enemy's prime weapon to keep us from intimacy with

---

[9] Finis Jennings Dake, *Dake's Annotated Reference Bible* (Dake Bible Sales, Inc. Lawrenceville, GA: 1987), comment "a" Genesis 2:25, 3.

God, peace with ourselves, and being the light and hope to others which furthers the Kingdom.

Next, recognizing shame in your life.

Chapter Two

Looking Behind the Mask

"Shame is a soul eating emotion."
C. G. Jung

It knifes through you. A glance, a word, a tone of voice, a gesture. Something is said or done by others or by you and you hope that the earth will open and swallow you whole. Right. Now.

Such is the feeling triggered when acute shame rears its ugly head. It grips you, the sinking feeling, the red face, the paralyzing inability to think or speak, the pounding heart, the dizziness, the nausea, and the strong desire to flee either physically and/or emotionally. Shame is a fear-based internal condition with feelings of being unworthy and/or unloveable.

According to Brené Brown, shame is "the fear of disconnection."[10] She defines it as, "the intensely painful feeling or experience of believing that we are flawed and therefore unworthy of love and belonging."[11]

---

[10] Brené Brown, *Daring Greatly* (Gotham Group, Penguin Books, NY, NY. 2012), 68.
[11] Brown, 69.

This fear of disconnection comes from the belief that something we have or have not said or have or have not done renders us unfit for the connection of relationship. It is our expectations and perceptions of who we think we "should" be—but believe we are not. The underlying fear is one of lack. We "lack" something which we need to truly belong. The resulting shame is a powerful form of self-judgment where we compare ourselves with others and come up short. In the core of our being, then, our belief of who we are, is distorted by the belief system that we are fatally flawed with no hope of redemption.

By its nature, shame is built in the context of relationship between two people. It starts as external, meaning it is perceived and received when another acts in a way that makes a person fear they are fatally flawed. Whether spoken or implied, the communication given is a "deficiency message," e.g., "you are not good," "you aren't good enough," "you do not belong," "you are not lovable," "you should not exist."

These "deficiency messages" come in many ways, one of which is being disciplined with silent disgust—the LOOK that lets you know you are perceived as "less than" and which feels like abandonment. Since we are "wired" for relationship, being or feeling abandoned is extremely emotionally painful. It reinforces a belief that we are so flawed, relationship and belonging is not possible for us.

Discipline which uses negative comments about who we are as a person rather than directed toward a specific behavior tatters the core identity of who God created us to be. Comments like, "You're a brat," "You're selfish," "You're a loser," etc. are directed at our personhood and heaps shame upon us. The truth of who we are, created by God, is GOOD! Our behavior may need to change, however our core essence hasn't changed since God looked on what He created and declared it all good.

Public humiliation by parents, teachers, coaches, colleagues, bosses, etc. sends the message that we are not worthy of honor. It highlights our supposed flaws for everyone to see. God honors us, never putting shame on us. Jesus paid for any shame we have brought on ourselves at the Cross. We must honor others as God honors us.

There are countless stories to share regarding public humiliation. Several of them center around very young children, first and second grade, who had "accidents" when they told the teacher they needed to use the bathroom and were refused. Then the children were held up to ridicule in front of the entire class. Again, there are several stories where bosses have thought nothing of demeaning and belittling some of my clients in front of other co-workers.

Though sometimes more subtle, being treated differently from others can be another source of shame. There are countless stories of children who were not wanted or step-children in blended families who were treated differently. How about classrooms or sports teams? As adults in the workplace?

A few of my clients struggled with shame and worth because as a child they had to ride the "short bus" (used for special education) in elementary school. Subtle or not so subtle, the message is that somehow you are deficient.

More difficult to discern is when, to feel loved and accepted, we must hide or shut down parts of who we are—

our needs, emotions, successes, mistakes, etc. Growing up in an environment where it is not safe to express our needs or emotions makes a child unconsciously learn that to keep the peace, to make others remain calm and happy, to survive, they must hide. Not to hide can bring retribution or open shaming from parents or caregivers.

Many of my clients who grew up in families with alcoholism or drugs have told me stories of needing to be the parent, taking care of the hung-over or "high" parent. They were also expected to care for younger siblings, so their needs were never taken into account. If they expressed a need, they could be mocked or at worst beaten for "wanting too much."

When others are jealous of our successes, we may learn to be ashamed of them. One story told to me was of a child who won a sports trophy but was forced to give it to a younger sibling. After that, he hid his achievements from his family and struggled to celebrate his success in life—feeling ashamed of it.

Certainly where there is an environment of shame, no one easily admits to their mistakes because of the shaming which will follow. Fear of what will happen and past experiences of what has happened when mistakes are admitted, combine to often set up a stronghold of lying in a person. People would rather lie than feel the fear and shame of having to admit to a mistake.

Another subtle deficiency message is being blamed for the emotions, attitudes and/or actions of others, i.e., "You make me so mad" or "I wouldn't _____ if you would just _____."

A client told me a story of her mother who was an alcoholic. The mother would leave in the evenings for hours or overnight expecting my client, who was six years old at the time, to watch her two-year-old sister. When the two year old became ill and nearly died, the mother blamed my client for letting it happen. Needless to say, there were layers of shame, fear, and guilt that Jesus needed to remove.

Constantly having the boundary moved of what will bring love and approval from others makes us feel deficient because we can never reach the "magic" goal. We do what is asked and find out it is never quite right. If we just do this one more thing... Nope, sorry, that isn't quite right either. You get the picture. The fear and shame which comes in this scenario often fuels performance and the striving to be perfect. If I just _____, then I can have love, belonging and approval.

Finally, there are few, if any, words of love spoken but rather words which tear at our being—"You have always been fat, ugly, etc...," "You will never change," "You will never amount to anything," "I never wanted you in the first place." "I'm always disappointed in you." Words like always and never create hopelessness on top of the shame which reinforce our "deficiency" and empower the lie we are doomed to remain as we are—fatally flawed and not worthy of love and connection.

Pause here for a few minutes and thoughtfully and honestly ask yourself these questions: Has there been (or still occurring) a pattern of...

1. Consistent messages of silent disgust—the LOOK?

2.   Consistent negative comments about who you are as a person (brat, selfish, loser, etc.)

3.   Public humiliation by others?

4.   Being treated differently than others?

5.   Hiding parts of who you are to feel loved and accepted?

6.   Hiding successes because of others' jealousy?

7.   Lying to hide mistakes out of fear of what will happen?

8.   Being blamed for the emotions, attitudes, or actions of others?

9.   Constantly having the boundaries moved by others of what will bring love and approval?

10.   Few, if any, words of love or affirmation spoken, rather words which demean?

Answering in the affirmative to any of these questions is a signal that mostly likely toxic shame is operating at some level in your life.

When these types of interactions occur regularly, especially with significant others, shame is then internalized and becomes hard-wired into a belief system. Any belief system, once installed, "runs in the background" without our necessarily being conscious of how it is affecting our lives on a moment by moment basis, waiting to be triggered. It becomes the "truth" by which we live and walk out relationship.

John Bradshaw in his book, *Healing the Shame that Binds You,*[12] identifies categories of shame based thinking:

Catastrophizing—a stomach ache means stomach cancer.

Mind reading—believing you know what people think about you (and it's never good).

Personalizing everything—if someone speaks of being tired, they are tired of me.

Overgeneralization—making one mistake then means I'll never learn.....

Either/Or thinking—thinking in extremes with no middle ground.

Being right—defending your position as right at all costs.

"Shoulding"—on yourself or others comes from trying to be perfect.

Control—Thinking you have no control or must control others.

Hyper-focus—on one element of a situation that supports your self-deficiency belief.

---

[12] John Bradshaw, *Healing the Shame that Binds You,* (Deerfield Beach, FL, Health Communications, Inc. 2005), 213-215.

Blaming/Global Labeling—Passes shame to others; makes global statements, "All drivers around here are a crazy."

According to Ronald and Patricia Potter-Efron, those who have an entrenched stronghold of shame are plagued with recurring thoughts—that inner critical voice judging whatever we do or say as wrong, inferior or worthless:

1. *I am defective (damaged, broken, a mistake, flawed).*

2. *I am dirty (soiled, ugly, unclean, impure, filthy disgusting).*

3. *I am incompetent (not good enough, inept, ineffectual, useless).*

4. *I am unwanted (unloved, unappreciated, un-cherished).*

5. *I deserve to be abandoned (forgotten, unloved, left out).*

6. *I am weak (small, impotent, puny, feeble).*

7. *I am bad (awful, dreadful, evil, despicable).*

8. *I am pitiful (contemptible, miserable, insignificant).*

9. *I am nothing (worthless, invisible, unnoticed, empty).*

10. *I deserve criticism (condemnation, disapproval, destruction).*

11. *I feel ashamed (embarrassed, humiliated, mortified, dishonored).*[13]

It is easy to understand how living with any of these recurring thoughts on a daily basis would be painful and exhausting. Just a look, an innocuous comment by anyone or one minor mistake on our part can trigger fear, shame and the replay of those deficiency messages repeatedly, continuing to trigger and heap shame upon ourselves. From the fear of disconnection, shame is activated leading to the behaviors behind which we hide.

Helen B. Lewis, a pioneer in recognizing shame with her clients argues that shame is representative of a whole family of emotions. This family includes humiliation, embarrassment, low self-concept, belittlement, and stigmatization. She sees shame as the core or root issue behind these emotions[14]:

Alienated	Different	Helpless	Inferior	Peculiar	Shy
Bizarre	Dumped	Hurt	Insecure	Powerless	Stupid
Defeated	Exposed	Inadequate	Intimidated	Rebuffed	Uncertain
Defenseless	Flawed	Ineffectual	Odd	Rejected	Unworthy
					Weak

If Helen Lewis is correct, when we identify those emotions within ourselves, it would be wise to begin asking

---

[13] Ronald and Patricia Potter-Efron, *Letting Go of Shame,* (Hazelden Publishers, City Center, MN, 1989), 14.
[14] Helen B. Lewis, *Shame and Guilt in Neurosis,* (International Universities Press, NY, NY, 1971).

the Lord to show us the root of shame, so that we can take it to the Cross and be free.

Shame vs. Guilt

A discussion of shame would not be complete without an understanding of guilt. Guilt is the feeling that we DID something wrong, not I AM wrong. Guilt is about actions; shame is about self.

Guilt is a violation of our personal value system where we understand that our words or behavior has created a problem. Inherent in guilt is the concept that a positive outcome is possible if we correct what happened.

Of course, there is false guilt as well. False guilt is taking responsibility for actions, events, or situations which were not our fault. One I hear frequently in the ministry room is people who have a false sense of guilt over the divorce of their parents. Another example cited earlier is of the six year old who was left with her two year old sister. My client carried the false guilt that she was responsible for her sister almost dying.

False guilt can be put on us by others and once accepted and believed, is internalized and then we replay the tapes on a continuous loop. False guilt is always detrimental and can be used to reinforce the shame cycle.

In contrast, with shame, the belief says there is not the possibility of a positive outcome since I am fatally flawed, therefore there is no hope to change.

One way to distinguish between guilt and shame is how you talk to yourself. What do you say to yourself about what is happening? "Wow, that was a dumb thing to do." (Guilt) Or, "You're so stupid. You never get anything right." (Shame).

True guilt motivates us to action, to restore the broken part of a relationship by repenting and making restitution in whatever manner necessary. Shame pushes us to hide, using self-sabotaging behaviors, further distancing ourselves from the possibility of authentic relationship.

Recognizing toxic shame and being able to distinguish it from guilt and false guilt is important. Knowing how to identify this elusive enemy is a first step. Another way to expose shame is by its effects. That is where we turn next.

Unmasking the Great Pretender

Chapter Three

The Effects of the Mask

"Shame corrodes the very part of us that believes we are capable of change."

Brené Brown

Spiritually

Toxic shame comes from the enemy's lie that we are "less than." We are less than parents, siblings, friends, colleagues, etc. with no hope of changing. In whatever way the enemy comes to us in the course of our lives to reinforce and amplify the lie, it affects us.

In a spiritual sense, carrying shame makes it difficult to believe God. Or if we believe in God, shame makes us hide from Him. If we believe in God and have received salvation through the atonement of Jesus Christ on the Cross, unresolved toxic shame affects our ability to walk in freedom. Shame acts as a "kinked hose" to the free flow of God's Spirit within us.

How can we believe in, be aware of, and receive God's goodness to us when we live with the stronghold of shame? A stronghold or fortress was built to protect and keep out marauders in earlier times. A fortress of shame gives the appearance of keeping out the emotional "marauders" but the reality is that it also keeps out God's bounty of blessing. Unabated, toxic shame builds a formidable fortress.

In response to fear and shame we build a stronghold to protect ourselves. Chester and Betsy Kylstra from Restoring the Foundations[15] calls it the Shame-Fear-Control Stronghold. From the fear we are not enough, we feel shame. That shame gives rise to the fear that if I am truly known with all my fatal flaws, I won't be loved or accepted. In response to that fear we begin to control ourselves or others by various behaviors so the "real, defective" me cannot be seen.

Shame can bankrupt us spiritually because we can never truly reveal or live from our authentic self. Fear that what we believe about ourselves is true—we are broken beyond redemption. We hide so long from ourselves that we no longer know or allow all that God has put in us— desires, dreams, and talents—to blossom. We become an empty shell, going through the motions of life.

Mentally and Emotionally

In *Healing Developmental Trauma,* authors Laurence Heller, PhD, and Aline LaPierre, PsyD, identify five biologically based core needs essential for our physical and emotional well-being. Their research highlights the core fear with the resulting shame-based identifications and pride based survival strategies. Looking at these core needs

---

[15] Chester and Betsy Kylstra, <http:// www.restoringthefoundations.org>

gives insight into the root fear and shame and its effects in our lives. [16]

Core Need	When Core Need Not Met	Core Fear	Shame-Based Identification	Coping Mechanisms
Connection: Capacity to be in touch with our body and our emotions Capacity to be in connection with others	Disconnected from physical/ emotional self Difficulty relating to others	I will die or fall apart.	Shame at Existing Feeling like a burden Feeling of not belonging	Pride in being a loner Pride in not needing others Pride in not being emotional
Attunement Capacity to know our needs and emotions Capacity to recognize, reach out for, and take in physical and emotional nourishment	Difficulty knowing what we need Feeling our needs do not deserve to be met	If I express my needs, I will be rejected and abandoned.	Needy Unfulfilled Empty Undeserving	Caretaker Pride in being the shoulder everyone cries on Make themselves In-dispensable and needed Pride in not having needs

---

[16] Laurence Heller, PhD and Aline LaPierre, PsyD, *Healing Developmental Trauma: How Early Trauma Affects Self-Regulation, Self-Image, and the Capacity for Relationship* (North Atlantic Books, Berkeley, CA, 2012), 3,5, 15, 40, 54, 66, 74, 84. This chart is a distillation of material from the pages noted.

Core Need	When Core Need Not Met	Core Fear	Shame-Based Identification	Coping Mechanisms
Trust *Capacity for healthy dependence and inter-dependence*	*Feeling we cannot depend on anyone but ourselves* *Feeling we always have to be in control*	*Helplessness* *Weakness* *Dependency* *Failure*	*Small* *Powerless* *Used* *Betrayed*	*Strong and in control* *Successful* *Larger than Life* *User, betrayer*
Autonomy *Capacity to set appropriate boundaries* *Capacity to say no and set limits* *Capacity to speak our mind without guilt or fear*	*Feeling pressured and burdened* *Difficulty setting limits and saying no directly*	*If people really knew me, they wouldn't like me.* *If I show you how I really feel, you won't love me.*	*Angry* *Resentful of authority* *Rebellious* *Enjoys disappointing others*	*Nice* *Sweet* *Compliant* *Good boy/girl* *Fear of disappointing others*
Love-Sexuality *Capacity to live with an open heart* *Capacity to integrate a loving relationship with a vital sexuality*	*Difficulty integrating heart and sexuality* *Self-image based on looks and performance*	*There is something fundamentally flawed in me.*	*Hurt* *Rejected* *Physically flawed* *Unloved* *Unlovable*	*Rejects first* *Perfect* *Does not allow for Mistakes* "Seamless," *having everything together*

From the chart above, it is clear that unresolved fear and shame have a tremendously detrimental effect on our mental and psychological health. The major effect is that we hide. The masks may come in different shapes, colors, or sizes, but they are masks just the same. We are attempting to control what others see and think of us, thus trying to dampen the shame we live with. We believe the lie that we are hiding our "fatally flawed" self from those around us. That may be partially true for a little while, however, we deceive ourselves much like the emperor and his new "clothes." [17]

This false created self acts out in ways that are "more" or "less" than human. On the "more" side is the protecting of our "fatally flawed" selves by controlling others, seeking power, attempting to appear perfectly righteous. Others can be treated in a patronizing, critical, blaming and morally judgmental manner.

One client I worked with was continually assigning motives to another's behavior without really knowing what the other person was thinking. It served as a self-protection for the client but was a cover up for the shame in their life. The choice to seem "right" was a deeply held belief system from childhood stemming from constantly being shamed.

The "less" side of self-protection tends toward the identity of compulsive failure. Acting powerless and weak gives a sense of control, getting others to do for us what we are afraid to do for ourselves. Degrading behaviors are

---

[17] The fairy tale of the emperor, deceived by a tailor, believed he was parading in resplendent garb when he was really walking around in his underwear for all to see.

chosen for which there is a continual self-criticism and blame.

Shame Compass
   Dr. D. Nathanson[18]:

Withdrawal

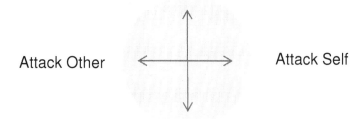

Attack Other   Attack Self

Avoidance

Dr. Nathanson's compass gives a broad stroke of behaviors which arise from triggered shame. He sees each point of the compass as a "library" of scripts (internal or outward) which are used to respond to experiences of shame. We either move away from relationship by hiding and silencing our true selves, move toward (but away from true relationship) by being pleasers or appeasers, or move against others by trying to take control. Whichever behavior or "script" is chosen in the moment is used to eliminate the excruciating pain of shame.

In her book, *Shame and Guilt,* Jane Middelton-Moz outlines the characteristics of adults shamed in childhood and how they operate in relationship to others as adults. See the appendix for the list.

---

[18] Adapted from Donald I. Nathanson, M.D., *The Many Faces of Shame* (The Guilford Press, NY, NY, 1987).

Not surprisingly, men and women handle shame differently. In general, the primary trigger for shame in men is appearing or feeling weak. Thus they perceive themselves a failure. Whatever situation a man may find himself in, weakness or perceived weakness pushes the "red alert" fear/shame button.

Results from many studies show that men tend to handle shame in two ways, by shutting down or with anger, and at its extreme, violence. There are those in the mental health community that believe shame is the core issue behind many violent behaviors.

Once a shame-behavior pattern is created within a man, the cycle reinforces itself with more withdrawal or anger, more shame over the withdrawal or anger, etc. Criticism and ridicule, sending a "deficiency message," either openly or passively, can initiate the spiral into the shame behavior pattern.

One typical behavior reported to me repeatedly in ministry sessions is that of shutting down. When there is an argument or disagreement, most typically the man will feel flooded with emotion and shut down his emotions and the discussion by stone-walling. That overwhelming emotion which surfaces and causes the reaction is shame. It can obviously be triggered by many different factors, but the root issue is the same, shame.

Women, on the other hand, tend to handle shame inwardly, with self-hate being the behavior pattern created. For females, the primary trigger discovered in recent research, is the need to feel or appear perfect—and not break a sweat (excuse me, glow). Perfect body, personality, wife, children, home, success in the workplace, etc. In short, women are to stay thin, kind, quiet, and modest.[19] Departing from the cultural "norm" brings criticism or judgment which ignites the shame-self-hate, more shame, more self-hate, cycle.

Generally, in the ministry room, women tell me they respond to shame triggers by working harder and trying to please. If I just do this better, if I'm just more _____, then everything will be ok. It is trying to find an external fix for an internal problem.

The effects of carrying fear and shame are highly destructive both emotionally and psychologically. Fear and shame keep us separated from true, authentic relationship, where opportunity to receive the love we were designed to have and invest in others is short-circuited. It takes us off track of our purpose and destiny.

Our Body Pays a Price

As detrimental as the emotional and psychological effects of fear and shame are, carrying them without resolution impacts our physical body and our health as well. Various studies demonstrate the increased health risks and of early death in those who are isolated and lonely.[20] Fear of being known and recognized as "fatally flawed" causes us to hide. In that hiding, we isolate ourselves and the loneliness follows.

Toxic fear and shame fall under the broad category of trauma. Trauma is a deeply distressing or disturbing

---

[19] Brené Brown, *Daring Greatly* (Gotham Group, Penguin Books, NY, NY. 2012), 85-91.
[20] Alice Park, *How Feeling Lonely Can Shorten Your Life.* (Time Magazine, Family and Health, June 19, 2012).

experience or experiences. Certainly repeated episodes of shaming either by others or internally to ourselves falls in that category.

In recent years a new specialty in medicine has been studying the relationship between how the physical brain supports the mind and mental processes. Another specialty studies the impact of adverse experiences on brain and mind development. A third branch has been studying how our behavior influences our emotions, biology, and the mindsets of those around us.[21]

Dr. Bessel van der Kolk, M.D., is a professor of psychiatry at Boston University and an acclaimed international leader in understanding and treating trauma. In his most recent book, *The Body Keeps the Score,* he states,

> Research from these new disciplines has now revealed that trauma produces actual physiological changes, including a recalibration of the brain's alarm system, an increase in stress hormone activity, and alterations in the system that filters relevant information from irrelevant.[22]

Trauma, then, leaves an imprint on our mind, brain and body. This imprint changes the way we perceive life and how we react to it. Under the fear of shame, there is a hyper-vigilance which occurs—always on alert to protect ourselves. God has always intended relationships to be life

---

[21] Bessel van der Kolk, M.D., *The Body Keeps the Score,* (Viking Penguin Group, NY, NY, 2014), 2.
[22] van der Kolk, 2-3.

giving, not life draining. When they are not, stress is the result.

God created our bodies to handle stress (from whatever source) for short periods of time—like escaping a saber-toothed tiger. When our body is in alarm mode, only what is needed for survival is resourced. Non-essential systems shut down, sending their energy sources to the systems which need it to move away from the threat. The two major stress hormones, adrenaline and cortisol, are part of our survival system. Both are necessary when handling imminent threat.

Once the imminent threat has been neutralized, it takes our body at least 72 hours to restore physiological balance. And, that is if there are no other instances of threat within that time frame. So one episode of anger, frustration, or deeply triggered fear/shame can only be fully resolved physiologically in that amount of time.

Further, every experience we have ever had is recorded in our nervous system (even the memories from the womb and before we could "put a story" to them). That system includes the brain, the brain structure in our heart (discovered after doing heart transplants)[23], the brain structure in our gut (controlling digestion as well as containing and regulating 95% of the keep happy neurotransmitter, serotonin),[24] and the nervous system throughout the body.

---

[23] Information on the "heart-brain" and its role in memory and emotion can be found at www.heartmath.org.

[24] Information on the "brain in the gut" can be found in *The Second Brain: A Groundbreaking New Understanding of Nervous Disorders of the Stomach and Intestine,* Michael Gershon, M.D. (Harper Collins, NY, NY, 1999).

Each memory has attached to it a neuro-chemical package. In simple terms, these chemicals are either stress or peace related. When an event occurs that is similar to a stored memory, the brain, part of whose job it is to keep us safe, searches its "files" for how that similar event was previously perceived. If the current event is perceived like an earlier event where we were not alarmed, then the "peace" chemicals are released and our body stays in a place of balance.

If, however, the "files" perceive the current incident as similar to a previously unsafe event, then the "stress" chemicals from that memory (and whatever other amount is needed) are released and our body prepares itself for survival. This happens whether or not you are conscious of the memory triggering the response. In many instances, the memory has been buried so deeply or occurred before language was developed, that your body will respond with pain or another reaction even though the memory cannot be accessed. Your heart rate and blood pressure go up, your breathing gets shallow, and your body is flooded to respond in fight, flight, or freeze—whatever will insure safety.

What happens, then, when the fear/shame (or other negative) memories keep recurring or we keep replaying them? Your body does not know the difference between the actual event and the memory being replayed. It continues to respond as if the actual event is happening in the present. Your body is flooded with the stress hormones over and over.

This constant release of stress hormones in the body, especially that of cortisol, over an extended period of time, literally begins to destroy the body from the inside out. This is because at first cortisol suppresses the inflammatory response in the body. Prolonged stress makes the body resistant to cortisol which then causes the body to ramp up an inflammatory response. Our immune system is overworked trying to put out the fire and begins to degrade. Organs and/or organ systems begin to break down, often times attacked by our own body, even the brain as cited above by Dr. van der Kolk.[25]

These long-term effects usually affect whatever body system is weakest in us. Correlations have been seen between long-term trauma/stress and fibromyalgia, chronic fatigue, and other autoimmune diseases like thyroid disease, Crohn's disease, ulcerative colitis, rheumatoid arthritis, and diabetes, to name just a few. Other stress related illnesses are heart disease (high blood pressure, high cholesterol, and other more debilitating diseases), asthma, obesity, headaches, anxiety and depression, gastrointestinal problems, and Alzheimer's.

In virtually all current medical literature on the topic of trauma/stress, there are documented correlations between not just the mental and emotional impact but also the physiological impact. Living with the stronghold of shame, which has the potential to be triggered numerous times a day, re-traumatizes and further impairs us. It is no small leap, then, to discern that when we are distracted by

---

[25] Two researchers from the University of Virginia Health System released information about their discovery that the brain is directly connected to the immune system by vessels unknown to exist until recently. This has huge implications for how the inflammatory response in the body attacks the brain. University of Virginia Health System. *"Missing Link Found Between Brain, Immune System; Major Disease Implications."* ScienceDaily. ScienceDaily, 1 June 2015.
<www.sciencedaily.com/releases/2015/06/150601122445.htm>.

either emotional pain or physical ailments, we are not able to be fully engaged in what God has called us to.

Chapter Four

Destroying the Mask

"When you hear the haunting melody of guilt and shame, drown it out with God's song of forgiveness and love."
Katy Kauffman

U p to this point we have covered the genesis of shame, uncovered its behaviors, and charted its effects on our spirit, soul, and body. Now, what to do about this insidious imposter in our lives.

As always, Jesus must be our example. Our salvation comes through believing in Jesus Christ, the Messiah and His finished work on the Cross. In salvation, we exchange our life for His. What is the scope and depth of that exchange? It truly is stunning:

> *Jesus was punished, so we could be forgiven. Isaiah 53:4-5.
> *Jesus was wounded so we could be healed. Isaiah 53:4; Matthew 8:16-17.
> *Jesus was made sin, so we could be made righteous with His righteousness. Isaiah 53:10; 2 Corinthians 5:21.
> *Jesus died so we might share His life. Hebrews 2:9.

*Jesus was made a curse so we might inherit the blessing. Galatians 3:13-14.

*Jesus endured poverty so we could share His abundance. 2 Corinthians 8:9; 2 Corinthians 9:8.

*Jesus endured rejection so we can have acceptance with the Father.

Matthew 27:45-51; Ephesians 1:3-6 (NKJV)

*Jesus was cut off so we can be joined to the Lord. Isaiah 53:8; I Corinthians 6:17.

*Jesus put our old man to death so the new man can come to life in us.

Romans 6:6;11.

*Jesus bore our shame so we might share His glory. Isaiah 53:3; Hebrews 2:10.[26]

Of course, discussing each point of exchange would fill volumes. Our focus will remain on the last point, Jesus bore our shame.

Jesus was utterly exposed on the Cross—the shame of being tortured, hanging naked, His reputation being mocked, abandonment by friends and seemingly the Father. Isaiah 53:3 describes the scene, men hid their faces from Him, the spectacle was so shaming. Hebrews 2:10 gives the reason for His suffering—that we, sons and daughters, might be brought to glory.

In the New Testament, the word glory (doxa) means an opinion, judgment, or view and is used there in the sense of a good opinion resulting in praise, honor, and glory.[27]

---

[26] Derek Prince, The Divine Exchange, www.derekprince.org.
[27] Strong, Greek #1391.

Jesus chose His suffering so that there would be a good opinion of us, resulting in praise and honor.

Jesus, suffered, took on shame, willing to be totally exposed for our sakes. Hebrews 12:2 tells us, He despised (to condemn, disdain, to think little or nothing of) the shame for the joy set before Him. What was that joy? You! You, sharing in His glory. His focus was on the joy, that even while He suffered and shame seemed to be winning, it was a fulfillment of prophecy. He carried shame to the Cross and it died with Him!!!

Romans 6:6 states, "...knowing this, that our old self was crucified with Him...". We are to reckon the old self as dead. It is no more unless we give it life. How do we keep the old self dead? How do we walk in the newness of life and not neglect the "so great a salvation" (Hebrews 2:3) paid for by Jesus?

Unmasked and Free

To walk in freedom from toxic fear and shame you will need to develop several skills. They will help you identify the fear/shame attacks and build the capacity to handle them in the moment using the truth of what Jesus died to give you.

I. Recognize—Since shame derives its strength by hiddenness, exposing it is a powerful antidote. The first step in any move toward freedom is to recognize and define the problem. This is especially important with shame. Take an inventory of shame in your life, asking the Lord to highlight patterns and write them down.

Inherent Shame.

From the Fall of Man in the Garden of Eden, understand, as a starting point, that we all carry inherent fear and shame. You are not alone in the human race or human condition dealing with these two master strategies of the evil one. He has used them since the Garden and because they are so effective he continues to use them. Grasping this one truth may bring a measure of freedom.

Family and/or Generational Shame.

Families can pass shame down the generations. When not recognized and confronted, it can be passed on physiologically,[28] as well as emotionally and through modeling. The roots can literally go back to conception and often goes back generations. This form of shame can be any form of abuse, neglect, substance abuse, adultery, ethnic hatred, religion, unwanted pregnancies or gender, perfectionism, harsh discipline, favoritism, persecution, etc. Any act of sin, rebellion or iniquity man does can bring shame, both to themselves and the others to whom they pass it along. Shame-based families have certain relationship dynamics described well by John Bradshaw.[29]

One family carried the shame of ancestors who were thieves. The prior generations were known for their under-handed dealings to cheat people. The current family was experiencing repeated financial setbacks which

---

[28] James M. Olson, Philip A. Vernon, Julie Aitken Harris, and Kerry L. Jang, *Heritability of Attitudes: A Study of Twins. Journal of Personality and Social Psychology,* 2001, Vol. 80, No. 6, 845-860; Copyright 2001 by the American Psychological Association, Inc. 0022-3514/01/S5.00 DOI: 10.1037//0022-3514.80.6.845

[29] Bradshaw, 62-63. See Appendix for the list.

brought shame since they were entrepreneurs. In prayer, the curse was identified and broken off and the shame attached to it. From that point on, their businesses began to thrive and they were treated with the honor due them since they were righteous in their businesses.

Personal Shame

Personal shame can come from our acts of sin, rebellion, and iniquity. There may be a legitimate reason for shame but it is only intended to make us seek God for resolution and appropriate what Jesus did for us on the Cross. Once we repent, we no longer have to live in the shame. Repentance is a change of thinking and a reversal of our course. Once shame is brought to the Cross, our thoughts about ourselves and our behavior must be disciplined to line up with the truth of the Cross. Otherwise, the shame will remain and become toxic. We may still have to live out consequences of our decisions, however the shame component is gone.

Ask the Lord to reveal areas of shame which you have taken on because of the actions or words of others. It may have come from their sin, iniquity or wounded-ness toward you. In cases of abuse it is usually easier to see. More subtly it may have been unintentional like the clients mentioned earlier who had to ride the "short bus."

Your Response to Shame

Each person's response to fear and shame will be different. Personality, life experiences, and depth of wounded-ness all play a part. What is important is that you begin to identity your unique responses to fear, shame and control when they rear their ugly heads. Many times, the responses are so habituated and hidden we cannot see them. Being intentional in rooting them out is essential. Otherwise they will stay hidden, unconsciously guiding your life in destructive ways. Again, ask the Lord to reveal your responses to shame--He knows where they are and wants you free.

You may fall anywhere on the continuum from shy and withdrawn to proud and aggressive. In certain situations you may act one way, in others, a totally different way. Again, observe patterns in the way you respond. Patterns are present and will help unravel the roots which set up the stronghold. Targeted prayer is most effective when you identify patterns and roots.

The Lies Behind the Shame

Wherever there is a destructive stronghold in our lives, it's foundation is lies. Lies can be so continually reinforced and strong they become the taproot of our lives. (A taproot is something which provides an important central source for growth and development.) There can be no abundant life and freedom where there is a taproot of lies. We know who is the source of lies, the father of lies, our enemy, Satan.

Therefore, the next step toward freedom is for the lies to be unmasked and exposed to the disinfectant of the "Sonshine!" It is crucial to realize that lies provide the structure and the root system which continue to feed and grow the destructiveness of shame. Without confronting and acknowledging the root system of lies, freedom eludes us. We may be able to quote lots of Scriptures, but until the lies are renounced and brought to the Cross, there is no place for the truth to take hold and grow.

You may already be aware of some of the lies you believe. Others are most probably hidden. Ask God to reveal all the lies which supply the roots of shame in you. Make a list.

II. Resist—Once the information is gathered, demolition of the stronghold can begin.

Forgiveness

Forgiveness is the gateway to healing. Jesus demonstrated His forgiveness as He hung on the Cross. He refused to hold onto any offense even in the face of unbelievable injustice and cruelty. His example is for us to follow.

Who to forgive? Anyone who has been, or continues to be, part of the shame and fear cycle in your life. As always, ask God to reveal to you who those people are. It may only be others but may also be yourself and sometimes God. Yes, I know God never does anything wrong, but we may hold a supposed offense in our hearts toward Him.

There are countless books on the topic of forgiveness (including my own).[30] As Christians, we know we are supposed to forgive. However in my experience during years of ministry with others, many people do not understand how to fully and completely forgive. Here is the condensed version that I now use in ministry.

Forgiveness has three components. In order to be complete, all three components must be addressed. First is

---

[30] Linda Forster, *Forgiveness: Gateway to Healing* (2013).

the decision to be merciful—deciding to release the offender to God without retaliation or revenge. This puts the person in God's hands for His justice and your vindication.

Second is the issue of what to do with the offense and its wound to your heart. *Aphiemi* is the most common word used for forgiveness in the New Testament. It means to forcefully expel or send away.[31] Whenever an offense has occurred, the wound has negative emotions attached, like shame, fear, betrayal, pain, abandonment, etc. To clean out the wound, identify and send away (forcefully expel) those negative emotions attached to the offense. Send each away to the Cross and wait until you feel peace come to your heart. You can ask Jesus to show you what He is doing with them. Once the wound is "clean," ask Jesus, the Great Physician, to pour His healing balm on the wound.

The last component of forgiveness is to repent for any ways you have responded wrongly toward the people involved or the situation. You are not responsible for what others do or say to you, but you are responsible for how you respond.

Repentance[32] may be needed if there was retaliation or revenge taken. Also, if another's personhood was judged, repentance is needed since God reserves the right as the only One to judge another's personhood. God called His creation of man "very good" and we are not to judge that. When we enter into that type of judgment, even out of our pain, we sow seeds that will be reaped in our own lives.

---

[31] Strong, Greek #863.
[32] Strong, Greek #3341. The word repentance in the Greek is *metanoia,* meaning a reversal or change of decision; a change of mind.

We either become like the one we have judged, we keep drawing similar people and/or situations to us, or both.

Aligned with judgments is the fact that we often make vows to ourselves regarding the people and/or situations. Statements like, "I will never..." or "I will always..." are extremely powerful in our lives. They can be so powerful that like one client I had years ago, she could not sustain a pregnancy for more than a few weeks. Molested by her grandfather, she made the vow that if that was what being a child was like, she never wanted to have children of her own. We prayed to break the vow. Six weeks later she had a positive pregnancy test, and carried twins to birth after more than six miscarriages.

Repentance of our wrong responses to people and situations who have shamed us is the piece which most people do not understand, do not bring to the Cross and most often why we remain stuck in our lives. Working through this third component of forgiveness cannot be underestimated.

Take time to get revelation on the judgments and vows which may be attached to the people and situations which trigger fear and shame. Repent for those judgments and vows. Ask the Lord to destroy them and their harvest in your life. Since unforgiveness, judgments and vows have the element of bitterness in them, ask Jesus to cleanse you and the others in your life from the defilement which bitterness brings. (Hebrews 12:15). Then ask for truth to replace the lies and vows. Write them down so you can renew your mind to truth.

As you work through forgiving, It is very important to understand some things that it is not. Forgiveness is not having to be "OK" with what happened, forgetting what happened, believing the offender will go free, or that holding unforgiveness will protect you. Also, forgiveness is not equal to trust.

Forgiveness is about the past part of a relationship. Building trust has to do with the relationship going forward. If there are continued shaming behaviors toward you by another person, it is righteous for good boundaries to be put in place. It is for your protection as well as providing an opportunity for the other person to demonstrate their true repentance and desire for a healthy relationship.

Renounce the Lies

With your list of lies in hand, utterly renounce them and their effect on you. Break agreement with each one in your spirit, soul, and body. Send them to the Cross. Ask the Lord to destroy the harvest of the lies. Then ask Him to speak His truth to you, replacing the lies. Write down the truth you are given. Let that truth be the witness (reminder) between you and God that the old has truly passed away and the new has come.

Renew Your Mind

Using the truths received from the above prayers, begin to renew your mind. Second Corinthians 10:4-5 tells us that the weapons of our warfare are divinely powerful for the destruction of fortresses and to take every thought captive to the obedience of Christ. You have the weapon of truth! Truth, given from the Father and Jesus through the Holy Spirit. Use it to wage war against the old ways of believing and thinking.

Nurture the truth by using Philippians 4:8, "Finally, believers, whatever is true, whatever is honorable and worthy of respect, whatever is right and confirmed by God's word, whatever is pure and wholesome, whatever is lovely and brings peace, whatever is admirable and of good repute; if there is any excellence, if there is anything worthy of praise, **think continually** (emphasis mine) on these things [center your mind on them, and implant them in your heart]." (Amplified Bible)

Brain research now shows that your mind can change your brain. How you think and what you think literally changes the physiological structure of your brain— either good or bad. Believing and living according to lies based in shame and fear, even unconsciously, creates stress. Chronic stress keeps the hormone cortisol circulating in your body and brain. Cortisol has been documented over and over to cause changes in brain structure and function (as noted earlier), even causing the "library" (hippocampus) in the brain to shrink.

Renewing your mind is a discipline, a training to overcome the old man with its mindsets. Not only that, but as Dr. Caroline Leaf (an internationally recognized Christian professor, therapist, and author) points out, the new findings in the area of brain research demonstrates how the "prescription" for reversing these unwanted changes have been in Scripture all along.

When you remove the unforgiveness, judgments, lies, toxic shame and fear, and discipline your mind to think on the truth, your mind begins to change your brain. It grows new circuits and strengthens the part of the brain which promotes peace and well-being. As that is happening, the currently stronger connections to the fear center of the brain begin to weaken and be pruned off. When you "Philippians 4:8" every thought, refusing to allow the old strongholds any real estate in your mind, you are on your way to much greater peace and joy in life.

One practical way to measure healing is to realize that once you have released the "negatives" from the memories (like unforgiveness, bitterness, judgments, rejection, abandonment, shame, fear, etc.), using the steps above, the memory will still be there, but the pain and sting of it will not.

III. Develop Resourcefulness

Since the enemy is so relentless in using fear and shame to target us, making a plan and developing resources to counter "shame attacks" is wisdom. Just because you have worked on rooting out the shame that has already been plaguing you, the enemy will not give up such an ancient and effective weapon so easily.

Because the enemy is not omniscient or omnipresent, his strategy is to set up a destructive stronghold through lies which a person believes. Once that is established, the person reinforces the stronghold themselves with the behaviors mentioned earlier. The enemy then sits back and watches people self-destruct. The key is to recognize the strategy and no longer partner with it.

When a "shame attack" happens, immediately pray and give it to Jesus. Refuse to partner with the old habits of self-condemnation. Ask for truth to set your heart and mind upon. Choose to give yourself the grace Jesus purchased for you at the Cross.

Because shame is empowered by hiding, another skill is to find a small circle of people you trust with whom you can be honest, open, and who will not judge you. When a "shame attack" happens, either being triggered by old patterns or by something current which happens to you or that you did, contact one of those people. Talk about it and have them pray for you. The very act of sharing dissipates the power shame has to control you.

When the immediate storm passes, decide how to righteously handle the aftermath. If it is something someone has done to you, forgive them (using the model above). Next, decide what boundaries to place around the relationship so that you are taking good care of yourself. Be willing to let the other person earn your trust going forward.

If you have done something for which you need to make amends, be a person of integrity, mature in Christ-likeness and make every effort to repair the relationship. There is a principle in Scripture called restitution. It is found in both the Old and New Testaments. (Leviticus 6:2-5; Luke 19:8). Whatever is broken needs not only to be replaced but added to by one-fifth. Apologize, ask for forgiveness, and restore whatever was broken or "stolen" whether material goods, time, trust, etc. and add one-fifth. This writes on your heart the cost of hurting someone. For the one hurt, making restitution demonstrates to them your sincerity and value placed upon the relationship.

Once I forgot my haircut appointment. "Shame attack" when I realized it. So I called, apologized, asked for forgiveness and rescheduled. When I went, I paid for the haircut but also brought a card with the money, plus extra, for the one I had missed. I had inadvertently "stolen" from her since she lost both time and money from my mistake. Needless to say, she was quite touched and laughingly said I could miss appointments anytime I wanted.

I cannot tell you how impactful the act of restitution is to restore relationship. The difficulty is to enter into it not expecting anything in return. Making this good faith effort does not always change the heart of the other quickly. If that happens, accept the situation with grace and keep your heart focused on the truth that you have made every effort to live at peace with that person. (Hebrews 12:14).

Recognizing, resisting, and developing resources to manage toxic shame and fear in righteous ways brings incredible amounts of freedom. Pursuing and destroying the roots, responses and the lies attached at the Cross removes many obstacles to fully pursuing your destiny. When the enemy's warcraft is no longer allowed to wreak havoc, you can have the internal peace of living out who you are in Christ. Toxic shame and fear no longer damage relationships, letting His life flow through you in healthy relationship to reach a lost and dying world.

Toxic shame and the fear which fuels it are powerful tools for the destruction of not only relationships but of our lives as well. On the journey to Christ-likeness we must confront and remove this stronghold from our lives. To live in denial of its existence, is to be hampered in the free flow of God's Spirit through us and our effectiveness in His Kingdom. Freedom awaits because of what Jesus has done—be courageous! Live the abundant life.

Appendix

Prayer to Break Shame Trauma

Father God, as Righteous Judge and Judge of All, I appeal to the Court of Heaven to hear my case because of the blood of Your Son, Jesus, which I have received as a propitiation for my sins. I request that Jesus be my Advocate and Mediator for this case. Thank You that Your books for me in Heaven are open and can reveal where the enemy has legal ground for continued torment in my life. Father God, with Jesus as my Advocate, please allow Him to call forth all witnesses who can present evidence for this case.

Spirit, soul, and body, I instruct you to be in proper alignment to receive from Father God the revelation for this case, to humble yourself before the mighty hand of God, repent as needed, and receive the healing He desires to bring, the blessings to be restored, and all goodness that is flowing from His throne.

Heavenly Father, in the name of Your Son, Jesus, I ask You to reveal the root cause(s) of the shame in my life. _____. "Search me, O God, and know my heart; Try me and know my anxious thoughts; And see if there be any hurtful way in me, And lead me in the everlasting way." Psalm 139:23-24 (Work on one issue at a time.)

Father God, I repent for each and every way that I do not and have not seen myself as You see me, how You created me. I repent for judging myself, hating myself, for carrying guilt, shame, and heaping condemnation upon myself. Please forgive me, that in doing so, I have lived with the lie that what Jesus did on the Cross is insufficient, that His blood is not enough, that His death did not render all those things null and void. Please cleanse me, bring it all to death in me, destroy all of the harvest, and cleanse those in my life from the defilement of my bitterness against myself. I repent for believing the lies about myself that came from others or myself. Wash away those lies about, give me a "single eye" to see myself as You do. Speak Your truth to me now about who I am and who You created me to be. (Pause and let God show You truth. Write it down.) Father God, I receive Your truth into my spirit, soul, and body.

Father, please forgive me for any offense I have against You _____. My mind knows intellectually that You have done nothing wrong, but there are places in my heart that have believed the enemy's lies—that You are not loving and good, but wrathful and vengeful. My heart has believed that You would not or could not protect me from _____, that You hear the prayers of others, not mine. There are so many lies I have believed about You. Please forgive me, my judgments of You and all bitterness which I have held. Cleanse my spirit, soul, and body. Cleanse the times, places, and situations where my judgments of You have allowed the enemy a doorway to torment me and the trauma of shame has "stuck" to me. Break the trauma bonds linked to these times, places, situations and people. I command the enemy to remove everything he has put on me or in me to keep me connected to the trauma. Bring this all to death and destroy the harvest. Cleanse me and those in my life from the defilement of my bitterness toward you. I repent for the lies I have believed: _____. Destroy those lies. I now receive Your truth. (Pause. Listen and write down the truth revealed.)

Heavenly Father, I now choose to forgive _____ who _____ (fill in what they did/what happened)[33] to me. I release that person/situation to You. I choose to show them mercy. I will not treat them as they treated me. I choose to give up all need for revenge because You are my refuge, fortress, defender, and vindicator. I cut off and send away the emotions of _____ (all emotions associated with the time, place, person or situation). Jesus, please come and heal the wound in my heart where those emotions have lived. Cleanse all of my cellular memory. I now repent for my wrong responses to this person and/or situation. I repent for all bitterness, resentment, anger, hatred, and judgment I have held. (Take some time to be specific.) Jesus cleanse me with your blood. Bring it all to death, destroy all the harvest. Reveal the lies I have believed because of this _____. I repent for believing those lies. Please cleanse me and destroy the lies. Please reveal truth. (Pause. Listen. Write down the truth.) I receive Your truth.

---

[33] May include: Abuse (physical, mental, emotional, sexual, spiritual), death, divorce, loss of a loved one, childhood accidents and injuries, surgeries, invasive medical procedures, frequent moves, major rejections, abandonment, accidents of any kind, major illnesses, attempted suicide, near death experiences, etc.

Lord, I confess, repent, and forgive my ancestors who
_____, causing the trauma of shame to
enter into and be attached to our generational bloodline by
their sin, rebellion, and iniquity. The shed blood of Jesus
and His work on the Cross took all sin, rebellion, and
iniquity upon Himself for all time. In repentance, I humbly
ask for cleansing of my bloodlines from the sin, rebellion,
and iniquity which allowed this trauma of shame to be
empowered. Please break the curse, declare it null and void.
I release the assignment of the enemy, and command every
device attached to the bloodline to re-engage the shame be
removed. Father, please release and restore the blessing to
the bloodlines in Your time and way.

Father, Ephesians 5:15-16 says, "See then that you walk
circumspectly, not as fools but as wise, redeeming the time,
because the days are evil." I ask that You open the book of
my life and that of my ancestors. Please reveal to me where
I or those in my family line have chosen convenience and
comfort over calling, where there has been the spirit and
stronghold of shame, fear and control. Reveal to me the
faithlessness of sacrifice to inherit our personal or family
birthright and inheritance by refusing to mature in
Christlikeness, walking in the ways of the flesh, allowing
shame, fear and control to bring a curse. Please forgive and
cleanse all sin, rebellion, and iniquity associated with this
curse. I ask You, Father, in the name of Jesus to remove the
Midianite curse off of me and my physical and spiritual
seed. Please declare it null and void. Please cleanse the
times, places, and people and situations, restoring the
blessing meant for those seasons in Your appointed time.

Lord, I ask you to disconnect me from all second heaven
entities whether principalities, powers, dominions, thrones,
rulers, etc. which have gained access through the trauma of

shame for the purpose of future torment. I ask that You remove all marks or markers put on me by the enemy for the purpose of identification and torment. Lord, would You seal off all pathways, portals, and any/all means of access for communication or influence. Would You free any parts of me captured and held by the enemy for torment in any time, place, or dimension. Would you cleanse, bless, mature and restore those parts to their original time, place and design. Please close, lock and seal the doorways to the enemy's domain. I further ask You to cleanse the time, land, situation, and the people involved, cutting the shame/trauma bonds to them all. I cancel all assignments of the evil/familiar spirits connected to this trauma. I command the evil/familiar spirits to the feet of Jesus. Go where He tells you. Do not return to me or my family. God, please restore the blessings in Your way and time.

Father, I now command out of me all short and long term effects, memories, and results of _____ (the trauma identified and prayed over) down to the cellular memory level and in every cell and fiber of my being. I command all shame, fear, shock, terror, chemicals (drugs, including anesthesia), poisons, and toxins ingested, injected or the body has produced or retained as a result of the trauma to be released. I break off all memories and effects of abuse, defiling touch, rejection, abandonment, curses/harsh words spoken, beatings, defiling activity from rape or homosexual encounters. I cut off all smells, feelings, tastes, sounds, vibrations and touch. I command it all to come out without injury or harm to my body.

Father, would you dismantle all triggers associated with this trauma of shame? Father, would you also restore the connections between the hemispheres of my brain, where I have cut off memories so that I could survive? God, I ask

You to reconfigure my DNA to Your original design. Would you now synchronize all aspects of my spirit, soul, and body to live in the peace Jesus died to give me?

Thank You, Father. Thank You, Jesus. Thank You, Holy Spirit. Amen.

Shame-Based Family Dynamics[34]

- Control or Chaos—One must be in control of all interactions, feelings, and behavior at all times.

- Perfectionism—Always be right in everything you do. Image is everything.

- Blame—yourself or others when things don't go right.

- Denial of the Five Freedoms—right to perceive, think, feel, desire or imagine. You must engage these in the guise of perfectionism.

- The "No Talk" Rule—forbids the full expression of any feelings, needs or wants.

- The "No Listen" Rule—individuals are so busy hiding and defending themselves no-one truly hears another's heart.

- Don't Make Mistakes—as they reveal the "fatal flaws." Cover up your own mistakes; blame others for theirs.

---

[34] Bradshaw, 62-63.

- Unreliability—don't expect reliability from relationships within the family. Don't trust.

- Don't Trust—because there is no reliability or predictability and no-one is listened to or validated, no trust is developed in self or others.

Characteristics of Adults Shamed in Childhood by Jane Middleton-Moz[35]

- Adults shamed as children are afraid of vulnerability and fear exposure of self.

- Adults shamed as children may suffer extreme shyness, embarrassment and feelings of being inferior to others. They don't believe they make mistakes. Instead they believe they are mistakes.

- Adults shamed as children fear intimacy and tend to avoid real commitment in relationships. These adults frequently express the feeling that one foot is out of the door, prepared to run.

- Adults shamed as children may appear either grandiose and self-centered or seem selfless.

- Adults shamed as children feel that, "No matter what I do, it won't make a difference; I am and always will be worthless and unlovable."

- Adults shamed as children frequently feel defensive when even minor negative feedback is given. They

---

[35] Jane Middelton-Moz, *Shame and Guilt; Masters of Disguise* (Health Communications, Inc., Deerfield Beach, FL, 1990) 43-67.

suffer feelings of severe humiliation if forced to look at mistakes or imperfections.

• Adults shamed as children frequently blame others before they can be blamed.

• Adults shamed as children may suffer from debilitating guilt. These individuals apologize constantly. They assume responsibility for the behavior of those around them.

• Adults shamed as children feel like outsiders. They feel a pervasive sense of loneliness throughout their lives, even when surrounded with those who love and care.

• Adults shamed as children project their beliefs about themselves onto others. They engage in mind-reading that is not in their favor, consistently feeling judged by others.

• Adults shamed as children often feel angry and judgmental towards the qualities in others that they feel ashamed of in themselves. This can lead to shaming others.

• Adults shamed as children often feel ugly, flawed and imperfect. These feelings regarding self may lead to focus on clothing and makeup in an attempt to hide flaws in personal appearance and self.

• Adults shamed as children often feel controlled from the outside as well as from within. Normal spontaneous expression is blocked.

- Adults shamed as children feel they must do things perfectly or not at all. This internalized belief frequently leads to performance anxiety and procrastination.

- Adults shamed as children experience depression.

- Adults shamed as children lie to themselves and others.

- Adults shamed as children block their feelings of shame through compulsive behaviors like workaholism, eating disorders, shopping, substance abuse, list-making or gambling.

- Adults shamed as children often have caseloads rather than friendships.

- Adults shamed as children often involve themselves in compulsive processing of past interactions and events and intellectualization as a defense against pain.

- Adults shamed as children are stuck in dependency or counter-dependency.

- Adults shamed as children have little sense of emotional boundaries. They feel constantly violated by others. They frequently build false boundaries through walls, rage, pleasing or isolation.

Characteristics of Shame-Based Adults in Relationships[36]:

- We lose ourselves in love.

- When we argue, we fight for our lives.

- We expend a great deal of energy in mind-reading. We frequently talk to ourselves about what our partners are feeling and needing more than to our partners.

- We pay a high price for those few good times.

- We often sign two contracts upon commitment, one conscious and another which is unconscious.

- We blame and are blamed.

- We want them gone, then fight to get them back.

- We know it will be different but expect it to be the same.

---

[36] Middelton-Moz, 91-108.

- We often feel that our partners are controlling our behavior.

- We are frequently attracted to the emotional qualities in another that we have disowned in ourselves.

- We often create triangles in relationships.

- We seek the unconditional love from our partners that we didn't receive adequately in a shaming childhood.

Bibliography

Books

Bradshaw, John. *Healing the Shame that Binds You.* Deerfield Beach, FL: Health Communications, Inc., 2005.

Breggin, Peter R., M.D. *Guilt, Shame, and Anxiety: Understanding and Overcoming Negative Emotions.* Amherst, NY: Prometheus Books, 2014.

Brown, Brené, Ph.D. LMSW *Daring Greatly.* NY, NY: Penguin Books Gotham Group, 2012.

Brown, Brené, Ph.D. LMSW *Rising Strong.* NY: Spiegel and Grau, 2015.

Dake, Finis Jennings *Dake's Annotated Reference Bible* Lawrenceville, GA: Dake Bible Sales, Inc., 1987.

Hawkins, David R., M.D. Ph.D. *Power vs Force: The Hidden Determinants of Human Behavior.* West Sedona, AZ: Veritas Publishing, 2012.

Heller, Laurence Ph. D. and LaPierre, Aline, Psy.D. *Healing Developmental Trauma: How Early Trauma Affects Self-Regulation, Self-Image, and the Capacity for Relationship.* Berkeley, CA: North Atlantic Books, 2012.

Kaufman, Gershen, Ph.D. *Shame: The Power of Caring.* Rochester, Vermont: Schenkman Books, Inc., 1992.

Kylstra, Chester and Betsy, *Restoring the Foundations Handbook.* Chosen Books.

Lancer, Darlene, J.D., L.M.F.T. *Conquering Shame and Codependency: 8 Steps to Freeing the True You.* Center City, MN: Hazelden, 2014.

Malone, Henry, Dr. *Shame: Identity Thief.* Irving, TX: Vision Life Publications, 2006.

Middelton-Moz, Jane. *Shame and Guilt: Masters of Disguise.* Deerfield Beach, FL: Health Communications, Inc., 1990.

Efron-Potter, Ronald and Patricia. *Letting Go of Shame.* City Center, MN: Hazelden, 1989.

Siegel, Daniel J. M.D. *The Developing Mind: How Relationships and the Brain Interact to Shape Who We Are.* NY, NY: The Guilford Press, 1999.

Smedes, Lewis B. *Shame and Grace: Healing the Shame We Don't Deserve.* NY, NY: Harper Collins Publishers, 1993

Strong, James, LL.D., S.T.D. *The New Strong's Exhaustive Concordance of the Bible.* Nashville, TN: Thomas Nelson Publishers, 1990.

Szalavitz, Maia and Perry, Bruce D., M.D., Ph.D. *Born for Love.* NY, NY: Harper Collins Publishers, 2010.

The Amplified Bible. Grand Rapids: MI: Zondervan Bible Publishers, 1983.

The New American Standard Bible. Anaheim, CA: Foundations Publications, 1998.

van der Kolk, Bessel, M.D. *The Body Keeps the Score.* NY, NY: Viking, Penguin Group, 2014.

Vine, W.E. *Vine's Expository Dictionary of Old and New Testament Words.* Old Tappan, NJ: Fleming H. Revell Company, 1981.

Articles

Caldwell, Robert D., M.D. "Healing Shame." http://www.psychsight.com/ar-shame.html

Fable, Jan Luckingham, MS, LADC. "Dealing With Shame." http://janfable.com.

Miller, Marc, Ph.D. "Shame and Psychotherapy." http://03435df.netsolhost.com/images/SHAME_AND_PS CHOTHERAPY.pdf.

James M. Olson, Philip A. Vernon, Julie Aitken Harris, and Kerry L. Jang, *Heritability of Attitudes: A Study of Twins. Journal of Personality and Social Psychology,* 2001, Vol. 80, No. 6, 845-860 Copyright 2001 by the American Psychological Association, Inc. 0022-3514/01/S5.00 DOI: 10.1037//0022-3514.80.6.845

Prince, Derek. "The Divine Exchange." http://derekprince.org.

Smoky Rain Counseling Services. "Shame: The First Great Barrier to Healing." http://smokyraincounseling.com.

VanScoy, Holly, Ph.D. "Shame: The Quintessential Emotion." http://www.soulselfhelp.on.ca/quintessentialemotion.html.

COVENANT OF PEACE PRESENTATIONS:

For seminars, workshops, or speaking engagements,
contact Linda Forster at:

linda.forster68@gmail.com
Or by phone: 717-648-4231

Publications offered by Linda Forster and Covenant of Peace Ministries

Loved to Life Manual –
A 16 lesson course on the basics of maturing in Christ. $25.00, plus $3.00 S/H.

Online Courses:
(Available at www.covofpeace.org)

Loved to Life 1

Breaking Trauma Bonds

Books

Forgiveness: Gateway to Healing –
$8.99, plus $3.00 S/H.

Perdón: Puerta de Entrada a la Sanidad –
$8.99, plus $3.00 S/H.

Vergebung: Das Tor zur Heilung
$8.99, plus $3.00 S/H.

Unmasking the Great Pretender: Breaking Bonds of Shame, Living Free!
$8.99, plus $3.00 S/H.

Make checks payable to:

Covenant of Peace,
16 Gunpowder Road,
Mechanicsburg, PA 17050